to the World's best

Grandma

edited by Helen Exley

EXLEY

Soft one

Grandma
you feel very
soft and smell
like roses
and your
skin is
soft
as
silk

COLLEEN MCKINNEY, AGE 6

When I fall and cut my knee she takes me in and laughs. I love her gentle loving touch, it makes me feel so safe.

KAREN WILSON, AGE 10

My Grandma has a look in her eyes like rubies and a gentle, loving smile.

CARRIE DOUGLAS, AGE 9

You're so good to me with loving touching hands.

LYNSEY BLACK, AGE 9

EIMEAR MCGEOWN, AGE 8

My grandmother is the best because she never lets me down.

ROISIN KELLY, AGE 9

She's the perfect woman for advice. When I'm sad she'll always be sitting in her comfy chair.

SARAH BREARLEY, AGE 11

I love you most because of the way you care for me when I'm ill. I love you for the way you sit with me and hug me when I've just come out of the bath. I love you because even though you are often tired you still come to see me.

LINDSEY BRACK, AGE 8

Always there

My Grandma she is the best, most caring person on earth, If anyone's more caring

I havent met them yet

LINDSAY MCINTOSH, AGE 10

LISA CLARK, AGE 7

REBECCA LAMBERT

She is the most happiest and Kindiest lady I have ever met.

CIARA MOYNES, AGE 8

The Kindest Lady

The best present you ever gave me was your kindness. You are as sweet as the spring breeze. You are as careful as God himself. No grandma could ever match your kind heart. There was no time when you didn't give me a good present. I appreciate everything you give me.

AARON MCCULLOUGH, AGE 10

When I am sick you are so kind to me, you tuck me up in the rocking chair with my crocheted blanket and then get me a nice, hot drink. When I am not sick you are just as kind to me.

HELEN HUGHES, AGE 10

NICOLA
FORBES,
AGE 5

Fun days

All nans do is ask their grandsons over to their house and spoil them to death. There are sweets being put into your mouth second after second so all your teeth fall out. They say it is halloween night tonight. As they brought you all those sweets so you buy her a rubber spider and she jumps out of her skin.

CHRISTOPHER DEADMAN, AGE 9

I go round to see her every day. She is always jolly. Every time she laughs her tummy shakes like jelly. She is nice and generous. Grandma also has an apple tart in the oven. And she has something for me every day and there is a lovely smell in her house.

GEMMA CURRAN, AGE 10

Keep me good

You are some times good and some times cross but you are always kind. Grandma you will help me grow up like a nice girl won't you?

SARAH AGNEW, AGE 7

I love you the most
when you say that
I'm the best girl in the
world.

SARAH
HUDDLESTON,
AGE 9

JODIE MCQUEEN,
AGE 5

The two of us

When times are hard you're there for me
You're like a secret friend
Telling me stories about when you were
at school
Making me laugh when you fuss about
Cooking me meals and baking me buns.

LISA MAWHINNEY, AGE 10

She always says who is this big boy
and she measures me on a bit of paper.
Then we have a cup of tea and bread
and buns. Just the two of us.

BARRY O'CALLAGHAN, AGE 7

MAIRE DOUGLAS

She is the sort of grandma that if you tell her a secret she will never tell anyone.

JULIA THOMSON, AGE 11

Every Saturday I vist my granny and we discuss what we did during the week. I talk to her about everything, she understands me.

When I am sad she cheers me up. and we have a laugh together.

MAIRE FEENEY, AGE 9

JOHN BYRNE,
AGE 7

Oh dear you live so far away I wish I could visit you every day

MARGARET STEWART, AGE 11

Sometimes I make you a card. I say "you put it on your table and when you get up you'll see it every morning and last thing at night before you go to bed."

JULIE COOPE, AGE 8

The only thing is I don't see her very often and miss her quite a lot but there are always pens and paper just to write a note. The phone is free for thankyous and birthday wishes too. The time of year I look forward to is Christmas and do you know why? Because I see Granny again.

KATHRYN COTSWORTH

RACHEL
DAWS

Twenty six again!

Grandma says she loves seeing us because we say she looks about twenty.

FELICITY ANDERSON, AGE 8

Grandmothers are supposed to be old
But mine doesn't think so.

HELENA HOUSTON, AGE 9

You should win the best Grandma prize
Because of your dancing, sparkling eyes.
Although you may be older than me
You seem to be as young as young
could be.

MARGARET STEWART, AGE 11

OLIVIA HYNDS,
AGE 10

Specially for you

When I was only four years old you knew that I loved classical music and you were the only one that gave me classical tapes.

ALAN CHARLES DUGUID, AGE 8¼

I am still waiting for the day when I get tired of your brown stew. It hasn't happened yet and I don't think it ever will.

DAVID TURKINGTON, AGE 11

My grandma sits in a chair and knits. Thank you for the socks. They're my best because they were made by you.

BRYONY HOWARD, AGE 9

for my Grandma

If I ruled the world I would give her two big fields of roses.

PAUL MCAULEY, AGE 7

When ever Grandma gets presents she always starts to cry.

KERRY MCMULLAN, AGE 10

CRAIG GIBONS, AGE 5

She'll do anything

Thanks for being a friend, a storyteller, a super cook, a handy dressmaker, a homework helper, a patient listener to tin-whistle exercises, a peacemaker, an understanding person, a television critic, a well-wisher, a gardener, a babysitter, a decorator, a shopping companion, a joke sharer or, in other words, a perfect saint!

ORLA MAGUIRE, AGE 11

My grandma doesn't make me eat my vegetables and when my parents have gone out of the room she eats my cabbage for me.

GEMMA BEEVERS, AGE 9

When my guinea pig went missing you got your legs all stung and scratched looking for it and you never said a word.

ALAN SMYTH,
AGE 9

ANNA WILLIAMS,
AGE 6

I love
grandma
because
She
takes her
teeth Out

BENJAMIN WILLIAMSON, AGE 7

KATHRYN YOUNG,
AGE 7

lovely and Old

Grannies are always very old at least 100 years.

EMMA DEVLIN, AGE 11

Dear Grandma, I love you for the hugs and kisses. You are sweet and kind. I love you. I love you very much. I like it when you snore at night. I like you being yourself.

MARY BOLTON, AGE 6

I love her. She can make sweets come out of your ear. I like it when she does that. I like her false teeth too.

KERRI BRENNAN, AGE 7

When my grandma is happy, I'm happy too.

DONNA MARCH,
AGE 7

BRIEGE AUSTIN

Happy Grandma

I see Nanny every Sunday. She's always pleased to see me. Her warming smile brings happiness and warmth in my heart.

TANYA HARVEY, AGE 11

My grandma has a lovely smile and smiles all the time when we are around.

LOUISE MAGUIRE, AGE 11

My Grandma is like he sun when it's dull she comes out and rightens up the day.

GREG MUNRO, AGE 10

ANNIKA CAMPTON,
AGE 6

My nanny is like a treasure to me and I keep her safe in a special place in my heart. Nanny has me under a type of spell to keep me good, it cannot be broken.

VICTORIA GRAHAM, AGE 8